C000002514

presents

THIS WIDE NIGHT

by Chloë Moss

First performed at Soho Theatre, London,
on Wednesday 30 July 2008

THIS WIDE NIGHT

by Chloë Moss

Cast

LORRAINE **Maureen Beattie**
MARIE **Zawe Ashton**

Creative Team

Writer **Chloë Moss**
Director **Lucy Morrison**
Designer **Chloe Lamford**
Lighting Designer **Anna Watson**
Sound Designer **Becky Smith**

24 November – 5 December 2009
Soho Theatre, London
Box Office 020 7478 0100
www.sohotheatre.com

Audio-described performance 4 December
Sign-interpreted performance 4 December
Captioned performance 5 December

3 and 5 December 2009, 4.30pm
Changing Your Story
Short plays by former Clean Break students

7 – 12 December 2009
Women's prison tour

Author's Note

Following my playwriting residency in HMP Cookham Wood, the challenge was not what to write about but what not to write about. Over three months I had enough material to write fifty different plays, each of which I could feel equally passionate about.

This Wide Night explores the importance and uniqueness of relationships formed in prison: how they can, or perhaps cannot, exist in another context; and also resettlement – when 'freedom' can actually feel like a very bleak and frightening prospect. Lorraine and Marie are inspired by the women that I was fortunate enough to meet and spend time with at Cookham Wood in the summer of 2006. This play is dedicated to them: Su, Vicky, Clare, Esther, Susan and Alicia.

Since the first edition of this playtext was printed, the play has been performed at Soho Theatre, London, and at the following prisons: HMP Peterborough, HMP Askham Grange, HMP East Sutton Park and HMP Morton Hall. Without doubt, the most rewarding (and nerve-racking) performances were those on the prison tour. This is where the heart of Clean Break's work lies.

Regardless of any similarities, or lack of, between the lives of the characters and themselves, the play was embraced generously by the women who saw it and their comments and input in the workshops that took place afterwards were hugely affecting and inspiring. So I would also like to thank those particular audience members, whose opinions mattered most.

Special thanks to the following for their help and support with *This Wide Night*: Lucy Morrison, Mel Kenyon, Jan Pearson, Cathy Owen, Patricia and Ken Moss, Tim Price, Mimi Kilgore and all the judges of the Susan Smith Blackburn Prize.

Chloë Moss

Cast and Creative Team

Ali Beale (Production Manager)
Ali has worked in theatre, opera, dance, performance and installation including national and international tours. She is also Production Manager and Co-designer for Fevered Sleep. Her recent work includes: *it felt empty when the heart went at first but it is alright now*, *Missing Out,* the original production of *This Wide Night*, *Black Crows* (Clean Break); *The Forest*, *On Ageing*, *Brilliant*, *Stilled*, *An Infinite Line*, *And the Rain Falls Down*, *The Summer Subversive*, *Fleet*, *The Field of Miracles*, *Feast Your Eyes* (Fevered Sleep); *Under Glass*, *Must*, *Performing Medicine*, *Sampled*, *Fantastic Voyage* (The Clod Ensemble); *Give us a Hand!* (Little Angel Theatre); *Guided Tour* (Peter Reder – Gijon, Arizona, Singapore, Bucharest and Moscow); *The Evocation of Papa Mas*, *The Firework Maker's Daughter*, *Aladdin*, *Playing the Victim*, *A Little Fantasy*, *Shoot Me in the Heart* (Told by an Idiot); *Gumbo Jumbo*, *Troy Town* (The Gogmagogs); *The Ratcatcher of Hamlin* (Cartoon De Salvo); *Oogly Boogly* (Tom Morris and Guy Dartnel); *Throat* (Company FZ); *Arcane* (Opera Circus).

Chloe Lamford (Designer)
Chloe Lamford trained in Theatre Design at Wimbledon School of Art. Design for theatre includes: *The Kreutzer Sonata* (Gate Theatre); *it felt empty when the heart went at first but it is alright now* by Lucy Kirkwood (Clean Break, Arcola Theatre); *Sus* (Young Vic); *Everything Must Go* (Soho Theatre); the original production of *This Wide Night* (Clean Break, Soho Theatre and tour); *The Mother Ship*, *How to Tell the Monsters from the Misfits* (Birmingham Rep); *Blithe Spirit* (Watermill Theatre); *The Snow Queen* (Sherman Theatre, Cardiff); *Antigone at Hell's Mouth* (Kneehigh Theatre and NYT at the Soho Theatre); *Silence* (NYT); *Lola* (Trestle Theatre Company); *Small Miracle* (Tricycle Theatre and Mercury Theatre, Colchester); *Blue Sky State*, *Soul Play* (Mercury Theatre, Colchester); *The Wild Party* (Rosie Kay Dance Company); *The Good Person of Sichuan* (Birmingham); *The Shy Gas Man* (Southwark Playhouse); *Holes and Wizzil* (Nuffield Theatre, Southampton); *Top Girls, Mother Courage* (Watford Palace Theatre). Design for opera includes: *The Magic Flute* (ETO); *The Cunning Little Vixen* (Royal College of Music); *La Calisto* (Early Opera Company). She won Best Design at the 2007 TMA Awards for her design for *Small Miracle* by Neil D'Souza.

Sylvia Carter (Company Stage Manager)
Sylvia Carter is a graduate of University College, London. West End theatre credits include: *Beckett*, *Passion Play*, *Vagina Monologues*, *Fiddler on the Roof*, *Semi Monde*, *Gigi*, *The Cocktail Party*. Other theatre credits include: major tours of *Fiddler on the Roof* and *Woman in Black*; shows with the RSC and the RNT; opera with the Buxton Festival, the Covent Garden Festival and on the South Bank. She has also worked in repertory theatre at Derby, Halifax, Leicester and Clwyd.

Lucy Morrison (Director)

Lucy is Clean Break's Head of Artistic Programme. For Clean Break, she developed and directed *it felt empty when the heart went at first but it is alright now* (Arcola Theatre) and the original production of *This Wide Night* (Soho Theatre, Live Theatre Newcastle and Drum Theatre Plymouth). *This Wide Night* won the Susan Smith Blackburn Prize 2009. She was formerly Literary Manager of Paines Plough, where she worked with many of the country's most exciting playwrights, including Dennis Kelly, Abi Morgan, Sarah Kane, Chloë Moss, Mark Ravenhill and Jack Thorne. Her directing credits include: *Product* by Mark Ravenhill (Paines Plough at Traverse Theatre, Royal Court Theatre Upstairs; European tour including Schaubühne in Berlin, and theatres and festivals in Moscow, St Petersburg, European New Play Festival at Wiesbaden; and the Bush Theatre).

Chloë Moss (Writer)

Chloë's first play, *A Day in Dull Armour*, was produced by the Royal Court Theatre, for which she won the Young Writers Festival, 2002. Her second play, *How Love is Spelt* (Bush Theatre, and US premiere at the Summer Play Festival, New York), was awarded a special commendation by the Susan Smith Blackburn Award. Chloë's other plays include: *Christmas is Miles Away* (Manchester Royal Exchange, Bush Theatre, New York); *The Way Home* (Liverpool Everyman) and *Catch*, a collaborative piece written with four other female playwrights (Royal Court). Last year, *This Wide Night* was produced by Clean Break Theatre Company and presented at Soho Theatre. The play went on to be awarded the Susan Smith Blackburn Prize, 2009. Chloë was writer-in-residence at the Bush Theatre in 2003, and Paines Plough in 2004. She then completed an attachment at the Royal National Theatre and is currently under commission to Paines Plough, the Everyman Liverpool, the Royal Court and Clean Break Theatre Company. Chloë also writes for television, including: *Hollyoaks* (Lime Pictures/Channel4) and *Lip Service* (Kudos/BBC3).

Zawe Ashton (*Marie*)

Zawe works as an actor and a playwright. She is currently Clean Break's Resident Playwright. Her acting credits for theatre include: *All the Little Things We Crushed* (Almeida Theatre); *Bay* (Young Vic); *The Frontline*, *Othello* (Shakespeare's Globe); *Play Size* (Young Vic/ATC), *Gone Too Far!* (Royal Court Theatre and Hackney Empire); *Rhinoceros* and *The Arsonists* (Royal Court); *The Cage* (Nuffield Theatre, Southampton); *Blue Moon Over Poplar* (Soho Theatre). Television credits include: *Holmes and Watson/Study in Pink, Casualty, Free Fall* (BBC); *Coming Up – Raising Baby Rio* (IWC/Touchpaper); *The Bill* (ITV). Film credits include: *Blitz, St Trinians II: The Legend of Fritton's Gold, Spiralling, Shooters.*

Maureen Beattie (*Lorraine*)

Maureen trained at the Royal Scottish Academy of Music and Drama and graduated with the James Bridie Gold Medal. Recent theatre credits include: *The History Ensemble, Richard III, Titus Andronicus* (RSC); *The Skin of Our Teeth* (Young Vic); *Small Change* (Sheffield Crucible Theatre);

Medea (Edinburgh Festival and world tour); *Ghosts* (Citizens' Theatre, Glasgow); *The Girls of Slender Means* (Edinburgh Festival). Recent television credits include: *Lewis* (Granada); *Midsomer Murders* (ITV); *Doctors, The Worst Week of My Life* (BBC); *Twelfth Night* (Channel 4); *The Bill* (Thames Television).

Becky Smith (Sound Designer)
Becky's sound credits include: *Cardboard Dad* (Sherman Theatre); *it felt empty when the heart went at first but it is alright now*, the original production of *This Wide Night, Missing Out* (Clean Break); *Frozen* (Fresh Glory); *The Juniper Tree, Reverence, The Ghost Sonata, Visual Hallucinations* (Goat and Monkey); *The Moonslave, Johnny Formidable* (Punchdrunk); *Seven* (Arc Theatre). Becky also works as a Stage Manager and Workshop Leader and has worked with Oily Cart, Paines Plough, Top of the World, Schtanhaus, The Comedy School, Polka Theatre and London Bubble.

Anna Watson (Lighting Designer)
Anna trained at the Central School of Speech and Drama. Recent credits include: *Plastic* (Victoria Baths, Manchester); *it felt empty when the heart went at first but it is alright now* (Clean Break, Arcola Theatre); *Rutherford and Son, Pub Quiz, Ruby Moon* (Northern Stage); *Glass House* (Clore Studio, Royal Opera House); *Something in the Air* (Oily Cart); *Sus* (Young Vic); *National Opera Studio Showcase* (Hackney Empire); *Twelfth Night* (Unicorn Theatre); *The Adventures of Wound Man and Shirley* (Contact Theatre Manchester and tour); *About Tommy, Richard III* (Southwark Playhouse); *King Pelican, Speed Death of the Radiant Child* (Drum Theatre Plymouth); *Can Any Mother Help Me?* (Foursight and tour); *Salt* (Ruhrtriennale, Germany); the original production of *This Wide Night* (Clean Break, Soho Theatre and tour); *...Sisters* (Headlong at the Gate Theatre); *Torn, Mariana Pineda, Venezuela* (Arcola Theatre); *Nine* (ArtsEd); *Stumbling Over Infinity, Tongue Tied* (Linbury Studio, Royal Opera House); *Songs of Grace and Redemption, The Time of the Tortoise* (Theatre503); *Critical Mass* (Streetwise Opera at the Almeida Theatre); *View from the Shore* (Clore Studio, Royal Opera House/Hall for Cornwall); *The Persian Revolution* (Lyric Hammersmith); *The School for Scandal* (Salisbury Playhouse).

Melanie Wing (Deputy Stage Manager)
Melanie graduated in Theatre Design in 2003 from the Royal Welsh College of Music and Drama. She has had a broad career working as Stage Manager, Designer and most recently as Prop Maker for the RSC. Her stage management experience includes: *Katya Kabanova* (Scottish Opera Company); *Odyssey* (London Bubble); *Hans Christian Andersen's Magical Tales, Othello* (Creation Theatre Company); the original production of *This Wide Night* (Clean Break, Soho Theatre and tour); *The Twits* (national tour); *Cenerentola* (Grange Park Opera); *The Lion, the Witch and the Wardrobe* (Leicester Haymarket); *The Jazz Conductor* (Sheffield Crucible); *Tattercoats* (Northern Stage).

For *This Wide Night*

Production Team
Production Manager **Ali Beale**
Company Stage Manager **Sylvia Carter**
Deputy Stage Manager **Melanie Wing**
Fight Director **Ruth Cooper-Brown**
Set Construction and Painters **Factory Settings Ltd**

Marketing and Press Team
Marketing Consultants **The Cogency**
Press Consultant **Nancy Poole PR**

Clean Break commissioned Chloë Moss in 2006. Chloë ran workshops in HMP Cookham Wood in 2006, at the time a women's prison, and her work with the women there was a starting point for *This Wide Night*.

Clean Break would like to thank the following for their support with *This Wide Night*: Cathy Owen and Jan Pearson, Maria Esposito at HMP Downview, Michelle Shanks, Fevered Sleep, Mark Ravenhill, Sophie Stanton, the women and staff at HMP Cookham Wood, Caroline Keely, Sigourney Weaver.

In the original 2008 production of *This Wide Night*, Lorraine was played by Jan Pearson, and Marie by Cathy Owen.

Clean Break

Clean Break is a women's theatre company set up by two prisoners in 1979 who brought the hidden stories of imprisoned women to a wider audience. Still the only company of its kind today, Clean Break has remained true to these roots and continues to inspire playwrights around the complex theme of women and crime. Integral to the company's artistic programme is our theatre-based education programme, which enables women in prisons, former offenders and those at risk of offending in the community to develop personal, social, professional and creative skills leading to education and employment.

Our artistic programme
Clean Break produces an annual production, based on an original new-writing commission by an established playwright, on the theme of women and crime. The production tours to theatres and prisons throughout the UK with the aim of engaging audiences and enhancing Clean Break's role as a social commentator on the subject of women, crime and justice. Over the years, we have worked with highly regarded female playwrights including Bryony Lavery, Winsome Pinnock, Rebecca Prichard, and Lucy Kirkwood. In 2009 Chloë Moss's *This Wide Night* for Clean Break won the international Susan Smith Blackburn Prize.

Our education programme
Clean Break has been running its Education and Training Programme for over fifteen years, working with women aged 18–60 years. The programme is delivered at our purpose-built studios in Kentish Town. It comprises creative courses, financial assistance and specialist support, leading to qualifications, increased confidence and self-esteem, theatre and technical skills and pathways to further/higher education or employment. The programme aims to create a platform for learning and engagement for women who have not been in education for a significant amount of time, or whose experience of formal education was very negative.

Working in prisons
Clean Break has developed an expertise in delivering outreach work in women's prisons. Alongside the production tour, Clean Break delivers theatre and playwriting residencies and workshops within each of the prisons we visit.

Working with young women
The *Miss Spent* programme has drawn on Clean Break's expertise to develop a gender-specific arts programme meeting the needs of

young women, aged 14–21 years, involved in or at risk of offending. Previously delivered in community settings, the programme is now being relaunched for young women in custody.

Make a donation and make a difference to more women's lives
Clean Break aims to bring about change directly in the lives of the women we work with and at a national level, by changing attitudes to women and crime through theatre, education and new writing. Our services are much in demand and we have ambitious plans for:

- more education work, affecting the lives of individual women and supporting them through their education at Clean Break and onto further or higher education, employment or voluntary work
- new-writing projects for former students of Clean Break and women in prison
- more commissions and touring productions focusing on women's experience of and relationship to crime, punishment and justice
- increased work with young women offenders and those at risk of offending
- training for artists and criminal justice professionals wanting to learn more about our ways of working

We invite you to contact us to discuss supporting one or more of these areas with a one-off or regular donation. We rely heavily on the generous support of our funders and donors. By making a financial contribution to Clean Break, you can make a difference to the lives of the women and their families. If you would like to discuss Clean Break's programme further and how you could get involved contact Lucy Perman MBE, Executive Director, on 020 7482 8600.

Alternatively you can donate directly online via our website at www.cleanbreak.org.uk

Clean Break   Tel: 020 7482 8600
2 Patshull Road   Fax: 020 7482 8611
London   general@cleanbreak.org.uk
NW5 2LB   www.cleanbreak.org.uk

Registered company number 2690758 | Registered charity number 1017560

Supported by
**ARTS COUNCIL
ENGLAND**

Clean Break would like to acknowledge the generous support of all its funders and supporters.
Clean Break is a member of ITC

For Clean Break

Executive Director **Lucy Perman MBE**
Administrative Producer **Helen Pringle**
Head of Artistic Programme **Lucy Morrison**
Head of Education (maternity leave) **Anna Herrmann**
Locum Head of Education (Learning) **Imogen Ashby**
Locum Head of Education (Student Services)
    Jacqueline Stewart
Education Manager (Accredited Courses)
    Vishni Velada-Billson
Education Manager (Short Courses and Progression Routes)
    Tracey Anderson
Student Support Worker (maternity leave) **Ella Bullingham**
Locum Student Support Worker **Jacqui Ennis Cole**
Miss Spent Project Manager (maternity leave)
    Jo Whitehouse
Locum Miss Spent Project Manager **Charlie Weinberg**
Outreach Worker **Elvina Whitfield**
General Manager **Louisa Norman**
Development Manager **Elly Shepherd**
Company Administrator **Molly McPhee**
Office Administrator **Sam McNeil**
Finance Administrator **Won Fyfe**
Administrative Assistant (Education) **vacant**
Administrative Assistant (Artistic) **Amanda Castro**

Board of directors
Joan Scanlon (Chair), Sylvia Amanquah, Jude Boyles,
Rahila Gupta, Sonali Naik, Kate O'Rourke, Sharon Shea

Patrons
Paul Boateng MP, Carmen Callil, Dame Judi Dench,
Sir Richard Eyre CBE, Barbara Hosking CBE,
Baroness Helena Kennedy QC, Ann Mitchell,
Yve Newbold LLB, Baroness Usha Prashar CBE,
Baroness Vivien Stern CBE, Janet Suzman,
Emma Thompson, Harriet Walter CBE.

THIS WIDE NIGHT

Chloë Moss

Characters

MARIE, *thirty*
LORRAINE, *fifty*

Scene One

Monday, 4 p.m. A cramped bedsit. One room with a tiny kitchen area and a door leading to a bathroom. There is a three-quarter bed on one side and a small armchair in front of a TV.

MARIE sits in the armchair staring at the TV which is on without any sound. A knock at the door makes her jump. For a couple of seconds she sits perfectly still. Another knock. She moves quietly from the chair and crouches by the side of the door.

Another knock.

WOMAN'S VOICE. Marie?

MARIE stands in front of the door, undecided about opening it.

MARIE opens the door. LORRAINE, dressed in a tracksuit with a thin raincoat over it, stands there. She is carrying a holdall.

They stand in silence, taking each other in for a few moments before speaking.

LORRAINE. Well, thank Christ for that. Thank God you're... alright. (*Beat.*) Are yer alright?

Silence.

MARIE. Yeah. Sorry I'm... I wasn't. (*Beat.*) It's a shock... surprise.

LORRAINE. I know. (*Beat.*) Your phone don't work no more. I tried ringin'. Some woman's voice comes on. Been worried about yer.

Silence.

Marie, can I come in?

MARIE. Yeah. Yeah yeah yeah, fuck... come in.

LORRAINE comes in. The two women stand opposite each other. Pause. LORRAINE leans in to give MARIE an awkward hug.

LORRAINE. Can I sit down?

MARIE. Yeah. (*Beat.*) Course. Yeah. Sit. Down.

Silence. LORRAINE sits on the arm of the chair; she looks round the room.

Take yer coat off.

LORRAINE doesn't take her coat off. She pulls a plastic water bottle from her bag.

LORRAINE. Can I get a drink of water, please?

MARIE. Yeah. Course.

MARIE stays where she is.

LORRAINE. I'm parched. Mouth's as dry as a nun's privates. (*Beat.*) Hike from that station, innit? Specially with that fuckin' bag. I could do with one with wheels. One of them fuckin'... wheely-bags.

MARIE stays staring. LORRAINE wipes her palms repeatedly on her tracksuit bottoms. An awkward silence.

You alright? How you doin'?

MARIE. I'm alright. Yeah.

Silence.

LORRAINE. Sorry, can I get that water? You could sand yer skirting boards with this fuckin' tongue.

MARIE. Yeah. Sorry. Yeah.

MARIE goes into the kitchen and fills the water bottle. She hands it to LORRAINE.

LORRAINE drinks. She is a little out of breath.

LORRAINE. Thank you. (*Beat.*) You look surprised.

MARIE. I am. I mean… it seems like ages away then suddenly it's in yer face – sorry I don't mean like you're in me face I just –

LORRAINE. No I know. I know what you mean. I feel like that. It's like a little… speck or something, speck in the distance and then…

LORRAINE wipes her hands on her tracksuit bottoms again.

MARIE. How d'you feel?

LORRAINE. Yeah, alright yeah. Bit… to be honest, Marie, can I say something? Is that alright?

MARIE. Course.

Pause.

LORRAINE. I thought… s'cuse me. (*Pause.*) I thought, coz you hadn't been in for a while, coz you hadn't written or been in for a while –

MARIE. I've just been fuckin'… really busy, Lorraine –

LORRAINE. No of course I know. I'm not sayin' anythin'. At all. I just thought you'd changed your mind.

Silence.

Which is fine, I completely. I fuckin'… I understand. But I just didn't know. I didn't know what to do. I got worried. I know you do that sometimes. You disappear for a while but I just had this feelin'. I had some sort of feelin' an' you know what I get like. I wanted to see you. See you were okay. I can go now I've seen yer okay.

Pause.

MARIE. This is what we said, innit? This is what… I said. It was my idea. It's just that –

LORRAINE. Well, this is it. This is it. That's why I – but that was ages ago. Wasn't it? So I don't expect.

MARIE. Thought you were gonna call or something –

LORRAINE. I did. I tried. Your phone's broke.

MARIE. I just thought you'd get in touch.

LORRAINE. I thought you would.

MARIE. I know, it's just been – it flies, time. Goes so quick.

LORRAINE. Yeah. No, yeah. This is it. Time flies on the outside. It's different, isn't it? I didn't expect I was gonna stay or anything.

Silence. LORRAINE *gulps the rest of the water down.*

My tongue feels like a fuckin' piece of Ryvita. Could I get a little top-up?

MARIE *takes* LORRAINE*'s bottle and refills it.* LORRAINE *takes a couple of pills out of a little fabric purse that she pulls from her bag. She swallows them with the water then runs her hands through her hair repeatedly.*

I won't stay too long. I got a whatsit… hostel. I got a hostel sorted.

LORRAINE *gets out a tightly folded piece of paper from her coat pocket, unfolds it and shows it to* MARIE *before folding it back up again and putting it back in her pocket. Pause.*

MARIE. I thought things'd be different. I thought maybe I'd get somewhere with a separate bedroom. (*Gesturing to the couch.*) They called it a studio. I got all excited but it's just a trendy word for a bedsit, isn't it? Studio.

LORRAINE. Is it?

LORRAINE *laughs nervously.*

MARIE. I sleep on this, it's a fucking fold-up, put-me-up fuckin' thing. Piece of shit. Springs go right up yer arse. You wouldn't want to stay on it.

LORRAINE. No. No no no. No way. I couldn't stay on that. Not with my back. (*Beat.*) I can't stay anyway. They're expecting me. I gotta sign in, haven't I? All that fuckin'… palaver. You wouldn't think I'm a free woman, would yer?

Twelve fuckin' years inside an' I'm still not free. Not properly.

MARIE. It's just a bit... one room an' that.

LORRAINE. Course. Course it is. (*Beat.*) I don't wanna be in the way. I thought give it a while then come round. But I couldn't. I couldn't wait. Thought maybe you'd been seeing him. Got back with him. Got into all that again.

Beat.

MARIE. No.

LORRAINE. Worried myself sick thinking about that. Thought he might be hassling you.

MARIE. No.

LORRAINE. Good. Good. Good. (*Pause.*) Only last time you come in, you said he'd been calling you. Said he wouldn't stop calling you.

Pause.

And I think it's easy done, isn't it? Easy to fall back into. You get out, you feel lonely –

MARIE. Lorraine.

LORRAINE. Can't blame me for worryin'... Thinkin'. (*Beat.*) Can yer?

Silence.

I'll have this and then I'll go. Marie. (*Beat.*) Just wanted to see you was alright.

MARIE. Yeah. I am. Thanks.

Silence.

You don't have to rush off though.

LORRAINE. No, I should, they're waiting, aren't they? Fuckers. (*Pause.*) I'll have this and then go and get signed in. Get sorted. (*Beat.*) Get going.

Scene Two

Monday, 5 p.m. MARIE *sits in front of the TV as before. The sound is off. She is still dressed in her pyjamas but has a cardigan over them. After a few seconds,* LORRAINE *appears from the bathroom. She has a towel on her head.*

LORRAINE. That's better. Thank you for that. I was all…

LORRAINE *goes over to the window. She looks out.*

Marie, what's he all about? Him next door with that… thing. What's he doin'?

Beat.

MARIE. Lookin' for treasure. Does it all day every day. Never finds nothing.

LORRAINE. What's he carry on for, then?

MARIE. He's a bit mad.

LORRAINE. You don't fuckin' say. (*Beat.*) Oh my days, look at him. Jesus. Some people.

MARIE. He lost his wife.

LORRAINE. Is she made of metal?

MARIE. She died.

Beat.

LORRAINE. Yeah I was… It was a joke. I was joking.

LORRAINE *sits on the edge of the chair and looks at the TV.*

Why don't you turn it up?

MARIE. It's broke.

Silence. They watch the TV. LORRAINE *laughs at something.* MARIE *stares straight ahead.*

Fuckin' mess. Sorry about that. If I'd have known –

LORRAINE. Well, this is it. You didn't know.

Silence.

You look lovely.

MARIE. I look a fuckin' state.

LORRAINE. You do not.

Beat.

Thought you were a fucking… yard brush first time I laid eyes on you. Body like a pencil, head like a coconut. Looked like you'd combed your hair with a leccy toothbrush. Now look at yer, all peachy-cheeked and shiny-haired. (*Beat.*) You look like an advert for Vosene.

MARIE. Shut up.

LORRAINE. They tried puttin' me in with this right bleedin' weirdo a few months ago. First I thought it might be nice, the company. She was a fuckin'… head the ball. Only lasted two nights. Tried to do herself in with a knee-length sock.

MARIE. You thought I was a weirdo at first.

LORRAINE. You weren't yerself at first, that's all. Coming off all that crap, getting yourself straight. I knew you wasn't a weirdo. Not a proper one. You were just a bit lost. (*Beat.*) Same as me.

Silence.

MARIE. You done all your things, all your forms?

LORRAINE. Not yet.

MARIE. Should've done them weeks ago. You gotta sort that. It takes ages.

LORRAINE. I could do with a bit of a hand.

Pause.

MARIE. They might give you a woman. (*Beat.*) I had a woman. Suzanne.

LORRAINE. They gave me a bloke. After you left. (*Beat*.)
    Brian. I wanted a hobby but I had to choose. Him or a
    pottery class. I quite fancied the pottery but there's not much
    competition between a wonky jug and yer mental health, is
    there?

    He was fucking useless. Made me write this list. Three
    things I wanted to achieve when I got out. I said number one
    I wanted to win the lottery and number two I wanted to get
    my son back.

    His fucking face. He goes, 'Well, I can't help you with the
    lottery, Lorraine, but we can talk about Ben. How old is little
    Ben now?'

    Little fucking Ben.

    I says, 'The little fella'll be thirty-one next June.'

    'Do you realise that he might not want to have any contact
    with you, Lorraine?'

    Speccy little cunt. (*Beat*.) Him not Ben.

    Anyway, he makes me write this letter to him. Ben. Sent it to
    this adoption place. He said sometimes it's good to write
    things down even if nothing comes of it.

    I just kept thinking I could have had a nice vase to show for
    six Thursday afternoons.

    Beat.

MARIE. What was the third thing?

    Pause.

LORRAINE. Come an'... see you. Keep in touch with you,
    wasn't it?

    Silence.

MARIE. I don't have to see her no more. That Suzanne. She got
    right on my tits. She used to put her arm round me when I
    sneezed like somethin' bad had just happened. If we were sat

next to each other. In the park. On the bus. I'd sneeze and her fuckin' arm'd come round and give a little...

LORRAINE. Jesus, I wouldn't want none of that. I just wanna bit of help getting some money, somewhere proper to stay. I wouldn't want none of that fuckin'... shit.

MARIE. You haven't got no choice sometimes. S'what you gotta do. Prove you're good enough. Show them.

LORRAINE. I'm not a performing monkey. What you supposed to do?

MARIE. Talk. Only I never said nothing. She did all the talking and I pretended I was listenin'. She used to say stuff like 'value'. Not like 'value for money', like 'personal value'.

LORRAINE. Fuckin' hell.

MARIE. And 'investment' – same thing. And 'strength'. (*Beat.*) She used to say 'strength' 'bout fuckin' fifty times a day. Fucked me right off . 'Look at that woman in that photograph, Marie. Look at her strength.' 'Eat some of these mung beans, they'll give you strength.' (*Beat.*) 'You've got such inner strength, Marie.'

LORRAINE. Fuck. That.

MARIE. She told me about this thing she used to do in college when she tried to be an actress. The teacher used to make them all do this thing called 'rock and cradle'. You go in pairs and you take it in turns to rock and cradle each other. Like you're little tiny babies.

LORRAINE. Rock and cradle? (*Beat.*) Jesus. If she comes near me... that Suzanne. I tell yer... Nobody mentioned all that. Nobody mentioned anything. I just got a number to call. This is all... fuckin' news to me. Fucking rockin' and cradling? Jesus fuckin' Christ on a bike.

MARIE *starts laughing*.

What's so funny?

MARIE. You are. You make me laugh.

LORRAINE. Do I?

MARIE. Course you do. You know you do. You crack me up.

LORRAINE. I really missed you, Marie.

Silence.

Jesus, listen to my stomach. Sounds like Battersea Dogs' Home.

MARIE. I'll make you something.

LORRAINE. No.

MARIE. Lorraine, you're hungry.

LORRAINE. What time is it?

MARIE. Five o'clock.

LORRAINE. I'm alright for a bit. We don't eat 'til half past.

MARIE. We could get a pizza. Pepperoni. S'your favourite, innit? Pepperoni?

LORRAINE. Is it?

MARIE. Yeah.

LORRAINE. Lovely.

Scene Three

An hour later. LORRAINE *is sitting in the armchair.*

MARIE *sits on the floor. There is a plate on the floor with pizza crusts on.* MARIE *drinks from a can of lager.*

MARIE. I only saw him the once. Just after I got out. It was a fucking disaster. As usual. (*Beat.*) We met in this pub and he kicks off coz he reckons I've been flirting with some old bloke.

We get outside and he's all, 'What the fuck was that about, Marie?'

You'd've thought I'd give this bloke a cheeky wank under the table, because he just crumples. He looked like a little boy. Crouches down in the road and starts crying.

Beat.

Then all of a sudden out of nowhere he stands up and starts booting the side of this car. Kicking the shit out of it.

I fucking hate the way he doesn't have respect for people's stuff. (*Beat.*) Then he's running off down the road like a fucking coward.

Beat.

I catch him up eventually and we end up running side by side over Waterloo Bridge.

I start laughing, I couldn't help it.

Beat.

He stops and looks at me. And he puts both hands around my neck.

MARIE *gestures*.

Just for a second. Then he climbs onto the bridge wall. I knew he wasn't gonna jump because he took his coat off like they do in films.

I go, 'Keep it on, you'll fuckin' sink quicker.'

He gets down in the end and we just sit in the road.

He said he loved me too much.

LORRAINE. Some funny fuckin' love.

MARIE. Yeah, well, I said. I'm not having it no more. He goes on about changing. Promising all sorts. He'll get off the gear. He'll do this, he'll do that.

LORRAINE. He won't change. He won't fuckin' change. Take it from me, Marie. Take it from someone who knows.

MARIE. I know. I said – I told him. I said come back when you can prove yourself.

LORRAINE. You shouldn't be encouraging him.

MARIE. I'm not.

LORRAINE. You're givin' him whatsit… hope. If he changes you'll take him back.

MARIE. He won't change, though, will he?

LORRAINE. He won't fuckin' change.

Beat.

MARIE. I just walked away.

LORRAINE. Good. Good for you. That's freedom that is. Being able to just walk away.

Silence.

MARIE. Lorraine, I gotta work tonight.

LORRAINE. That's alright.

MARIE. I fuckin'… hate it.

Beat.

My boss is eighteen, can you get onto that? I'm standing there taking shit off a spotty little twat nearly young enough to be me son. He goes, 'You gotta pull your socks up, Marie.' I go, 'Is it Tinky Winky, yeah? I gotta pull my socks up, yeah? I'll be pulling something right up pretty soon but it won't be my fucking socks, mate.' (*Beat.*) I didn't say that but I wanted to. Are you sure you don't wanna beer, Lorraine?

Silence.

LORRAINE. No thanks.

MARIE. I wouldn't go in but I've got to. I need the money.

LORRAINE. You need the money, of course you do.

Silence.

MARIE. You'll be alright y'know, Lorraine.

LORRAINE. Will I?

MARIE. Yeah. (*Beat.*) Course you will.

Silence.

LORRAINE. It was so hard after you went, Marie. I didn't say much when you used to come in because I was just wanting to get on with it but God it did me in. My little mate leaving me. Sorry.

LORRAINE *looks as if she is about to cry. She breathes in deeply and rubs her face with her hands.*

Sorry. Sorry, sorry. Sorry. (*Beat.*) Fuck.

MARIE. Oh, c'mon.

LORRAINE. No I know. I'm alright. (*Beat.*) Sorry.

MARIE. Stop it, stop sayin' sorry.

LORRAINE. Okay. Alright.

Silence. LORRAINE *takes deep breaths.*

MARIE. If you want to stay here. For tonight.

LORRAINE. No –

MARIE. You can do. It's alright. (*Beat.*) It's fine.

Pause.

LORRAINE. That'd be… just for tonight. It'd be –

MARIE. I gotta work though, Lorraine.

LORRAINE. Course you have.

MARIE. You'll be alright? On your own for a while?

LORRAINE. Course I will. Just for tonight. (*Beat.*) I'd like that.

Scene Four

Tuesday, 2.30 a.m. LORRAINE *is asleep on the bed. After a few moments the door opens and* MARIE *enters. She gets undressed hurriedly.* LORRAINE *stirs.*

LORRAINE. What time is it?

MARIE. I dunno.

LORRAINE. It's half two.

> MARIE *heads to the bathroom and gets into the shower.* LORRAINE *gets out of bed and puts the light on. She gets her tablets from her bag, takes two then gets back into bed.* LORRAINE *lies down.*

> *Silence.*

> I watched a film. (*Beat.*) You get used to it, don't yer? Without the sound.

MARIE. What?

LORRAINE (*shouting, loudly*). I watched a film, you get used to it without the sound.

> MARIE *appears a towel wrapped around her.*

> Sorry.

> MARIE *gets a T-shirt from her drawer and goes back into the bathroom. She comes out wearing it with the towel wrapped around her head.*

> They keep you late at that place, don't they?

MARIE. Stayed behind. Had a few drinks.

LORRAINE. I couldn't sleep.

> *Silence.*

> Kept tossing and turning. I dropped off eventually but then you come in.

MARIE *sits on the edge of the bed, towel-drying her hair.*

I'm not so good lately. Sleeping. Any little noise and that's it then. Wide awake. I never used to be like that, did I? You were like that. Pacing about, night after night. The more you think about it, the worse it gets. (*Beat.*) I've been like this a few weeks now. (*Pause.*) Reading helps, having a little read.

Silence. MARIE *turns the light off and gets into bed.*

Marie?

MARIE. Mmm.

LORRAINE. D'you mind if I have a little read? (*Beat.*) I don't mean putting the big light on. I've got me torch.

MARIE. No.

Pause.

LORRAINE. Do you mean no I can't or no you don't mind?

MARIE. No I don't mind.

LORRAINE. Ta.

LORRAINE *reaches into her bag which is at the side of the bed and pulls out a torch and a book. She starts to read, whispering the words under her breath.*

MARIE. Lorraine.

LORRAINE. Yeah?

MARIE. Can you read in your head, please?

LORRAINE. Sorry. (*Beat.*) Night.

LORRAINE *reaches over and pats* MARIE*'s head.*

MARIE. Can you not shine that right in my face?

LORRAINE. Sorry,

LORRAINE *flicks through the book, a small folded piece of paper falls out.* LORRAINE *retrieves it from the bedclothes.*

MARIE. Who's that from?

Beat.

LORRAINE. Ben. When he was little. It's falling to pieces now. I like the smell of it.

LORRAINE *sniffs the letter than places it carefully inside the book and shoves it back under her pillow.* MARIE *turns on her side to sleep as* LORRAINE *starts making shadow shapes with her hand.*

What's that?

MARIE. A duck.

LORRAINE. You're not even lookin'.

MARIE. It's always a duck. You can't do nothing else.

A long silence. The rain beats at the window.

LORRAINE. Listen to that. S'like someone chucking golfballs at the window. D'you know what it reminds me of?

MARIE. My first night. (*Beat.*) I thought you was a nutter at first.

LORRAINE. Why?

MARIE. Goin' on about meditating to the sound of the fuckin' rain. I'm practically scratching at the walls, and you're just lying there. Then you go, 'The silence takes a bit of gettin' used to. You listen to your heart beatin' and you listen to yourself breathing and when it rains it sounds deafening.'

LORRAINE. I never said that. Did I say that? That sounds quite... I like that.

Silence. MARIE *stands and opens the curtains.*

MARIE. D'you mind? I can't sleep either.

LORRAINE. You've gone past it probably.

MARIE. Helps if I have the curtains open.

MARIE *gets back into bed. She lies down and* LORRAINE
starts to stroke her head with one hand.

I used to do this thing when I was little. Raindrop racing. I'd
fix on two drops. One would be me and the other one would
be any kid in school who was doing alright, like if they had a
nice mum and dad or a nice house.

Mostly it was Charlotte Hughes coz her mum worked in
Greggs and put cream cakes in her packed lunch.

Sometimes my one'd stop and hang on another raindrop and
I'd imagine that was when I went to stay with Aunty Barbara
or Mr and Mrs Dent or Sam and Jason's then it'd separate
and roll down and catch up with Charlotte Hughes.

Aim of the game was that if you got down first then you'd be
alright.

Aunty Barbara, she weren't my proper aunty but she made
me call her that for some reason, she used to say, 'Not
everyone can be alright, Marie. The world isn't like that.
Some people are rich and some people are poor and some
people's mothers work in Greggs and some don't. Not
everyone can be alright. That isn't how things work.'

I didn't have anything against Charlotte Hughes.

She used to break off bits of cake when I asked for a bit. But
I weren't allowed to take a bite. She'd go, 'You've always
got cold sores, Marie, and once you catch one you've got
herpes for life.'

So I used to have me nose pressed against the window
willing myself to stop hanging about and get down to the
finish line.

Charlotte's raindrop usually zig-zagged along no sweat but if
she did brush against another one I reckoned it'd be
something nice like popping into a friend's for tea then she'd
be on her way, holding one of them party bags with flumps
and fruit-salad chews in it.

Once, David Harper was the other raindrop because he had a nan who knitted clothes for his action men.

Beat.

I still do it now sometimes. That game.

Silence. LORRAINE *has started to snore quietly.*

Lorraine? (*Beat.*) Lol.

Scene Five

Tuesday, 10.30 a.m. MARIE *is asleep.* LORRAINE *stands over her.*

LORRAINE. Marie.

Silence.

Marie.

Silence.

Marie.

Silence.

Marie.

Beat.

MARIE. Mmm.

LORRAINE. D'you wanna cup of tea?

Pause.

MARIE. No.

LORRAINE. You sure?

Silence.

Marie?

MARIE. What?

LORRAINE. You sure you don't wanna cuppa?

MARIE. Yeah.

Pause.

LORRAINE. It's half ten.

Silence.

Marie?

MARIE *makes an exasperated screech, pulls the covers off herself and sits up.*

MARIE. Fuckin' hell… I forgot about this… you fuckin'… rabbittin' on first thing.

LORRAINE. Sorry. You need time to 'readjust', don't yer? In the mornings.

Silence.

MARIE *lies back down on the bed.* LORRAINE *looks out the window.*

Metal Mickey's going inside.

MARIE. *Cash in the Attic*'ll be starting.

LORRAINE. Well, he can't be that demented with grief, can he? I had respect for him when I thought he dedicated every waking minute to walking round in a circle looking for lost treasure. Didn't know he popped in to watch the fuckin' telly when he got a bit fed up.

MARIE. I'm gonna have to leave soon, Lorraine.

LORRAINE. We can leave together.

Pause.

MARIE. I go the opposite way.

LORRAINE. Right.

MARIE *gets up and starts collecting items of her 'work outfit'. She goes into the bathroom.*

LORRAINE. Here, I was thinkin' before. When was the last time you had a holiday?

MARIE. Three years ago to HMP Cookham Wood.

LORRAINE. Seriously.

MARIE. I don't know. When I was at Poppy Lodge probably. I was about fifteen. Some of us got taken to Bangor. They sent me back early for nicking a bag from Dorothy Perkins.

MARIE *potters around as* LORRAINE *speaks; brushing her hair and putting lipstick and mascara on.*

LORRAINE. I've never been on holiday. I'm fifty this year.

MARIE. Not even when you were a kid.

LORRAINE. Specially not when I was a kid. Days out, I've been on days out. S'not a holiday, is it? Fuckin' poxy day out.

Silence.

Anyway, what d'yer reckon? Little holiday. Me and you.

MARIE. You won't be allowed, Lorraine. They won't let yer.

LORRAINE. Just a few days. Brighton. Somethin' like that. Somewhere by the sea. Sticking me feet in the water.

Beat.

MARIE. Train on its own'll be about thirty quid.

LORRAINE. We could get the coach. Stay in a little B&B. I got a bit put aside. Been saving. Got just over three hundred quid.

MARIE. Well, you don't wanna blow it all, do yer? Soon as you get out.

LORRAINE. I'll get a job.

Silence.

What?

MARIE. It might be a bit hard that's all.

LORRAINE. Oh, I know that. I know that. It won't be easy. (*Beat.*) I haven't got any qualifications.

MARIE. And you've just got out of prison. I don't wanna piss on your bonfire, Lorraine.

LORRAINE. No I know. It's gonna be hard. I'm not stupid. I was thinking of doing a course. What courses do they do these days?

MARIE. They do all sorts, don't they? You gotta decide what you're interested in first.

Pause.

LORRAINE. Y'know that book I'm reading. *Space: The Final Frontier.* It's fuckin' mental. The mad girl left it.

LORRAINE *goes and gets the book from her bag. She hands it to* MARIE. MARIE *studies it.*

Can I tell you something?

Silence.

You know on your telly?

MARIE. My particular telly or any old telly.

LORRAINE. Any old telly. (*Beat.*) You know when you're in between channels or the reception's really bad. When it's just like a black-and-white fuzzy sort of blizzard. You know what I mean?

MARIE. Yes.

LORRAINE. That's only the fucking big bang.

MARIE *looks blankly.*

As in, when the world started.

MARIE. Yeah, I know what the big bang is.

LORRAINE. Yeah, well, this is it. The big bang. On your fucking telly. Remnants of it from outer space. Millions of

light years away. I've highlighted it, it's in the middle
somewhere. Have a look.

MARIE *drops the book down*.

It blows my mind, that.

MARIE. What's it got to do with you getting a job?

LORRAINE. I dunno, I just thought about it when you asked
what I was interested in.

MARIE. You thinking about becoming an astronaut?

LORRAINE. No. Course not.

MARIE. You should take that book down to the job centre.
Show them the bits you've highlighted. See what they've got.

Silence.

LORRAINE. What about your work?

MARIE. What about it?

LORRAINE. Do they need anyone?

Pause.

MARIE. I dunno.

Silence.

I don't think they do but I could ask.

LORRAINE. Could yer?

MARIE. I don't think they need anyone but I'll ask, yeah.

LORRAINE. That'd be great that... that'd be –

MARIE. They probably don't need anyone.

LORRAINE. No. (*Beat*.) I could come in and see you maybe
when yer workin'... they could get to know me, know my face.

MARIE. I don't think – they might get funny about you...
distracting me. When I'm workin'.

LORRAINE. I wouldn't wanna get you in trouble.

MARIE. I'll ask though. About a job.

Beat. MARIE *puts her coat on.*

MARIE. I've gotta go now, Lorraine.

LORRAINE. Alright.

LORRAINE *stays where she is.*

MARIE. I've got to double lock the door.

LORRAINE. Right. Yeah. Sorry. Course.

LORRAINE *picks up her bag.*

MARIE. Got directions and everything.

LORRAINE. I think so – yeah yeah yeah. I'll be fine.

MARIE. I'd walk you to the station but –

LORRAINE. You go the opposite way.

MARIE. They get so arsey about timekeeping.

LORRAINE *hugs* MARIE.

LORRAINE. You look lovely.

MARIE. Give us a ring. We can do something soon, yeah?

LORRAINE. Yeah. (*Pause.*) What about your phone?

MARIE. Shit, right. Yeah.

Pause.

LORRAINE. Oh, hang on.

LORRAINE *fishes the hostel address and phone number out of her pocket. She hands it to* MARIE.

Phone number on there.

MARIE. Perfect. I'll call yer.

LORRAINE. When?

Beat.

MARIE. Few days.

LORRAINE. Lovely.

> MARIE *opens the door.* LORRAINE *goes out first then*
> MARIE *shuts the door behind her. After a few seconds the*
> *door to the flat opens again and* MARIE *comes in. She goes*
> *over to the window and peeks out before kicking her shoes*
> *off and sitting down in the chair. She lights a cigarette.*

Scene Six

Tuesday, evening. MARIE *sits, smoking, in front of the TV.*
There is a loud knock at the door and she jumps. She sits
perfectly still, rigid in the seat. The knock comes again,
followed by LORRAINE*'s voice.*

LORRAINE. Marie?

> MARIE *stands and opens the door.* LORRAINE *is visibly*
> *agitated and jumpy.*

MARIE. Fuckin' hell, Lorraine.

LORRAINE. Oh, thank God. I thought you might be at work.

MARIE. I shit meself.

LORRAINE. Sorry. I couldn't ring you, though, could I?

> LORRAINE *comes in. She is carrying a plastic bag. She*
> *pulls her water bottle out of it.*

Can I get a glass of water, please?

MARIE. What's happened?

LORRAINE. I'm thirsty.

> MARIE *goes to get the water.* LORRAINE *takes an*
> *envelope out of the bag and puts it on the arm of the chair.*

MARIE *comes back with the water and hands it to*
LORRAINE *who takes two tablets out of her pocket and*
swallows them with the water.

MARIE. Was everything okay?

LORRAINE. Yeah. They don't really give a shit, do they?
(*Beat.*) They looked at me like I was a turd. I got that. (*Beat.*)
It was there when I got there. Waiting for me. It's a letter.

MARIE. Yeah, I can see that. Who from?

LORRAINE. I haven't opened it.

MARIE. Why not?

Silence.

Open it.

LORRAINE. My heart... Listen to that.

LORRAINE *puts* MARIE*'s hand on her chest.*

MARIE. You don't even know what it is yet.

LORRAINE. It's handwritten.

MARIE. So?

LORRAINE. Official things. They've always got a little
window. And then inside the window, it's typed. (*Beat.*) This
is off a person, Marie.

MARIE. Course it's off a fucking person.

LORRAINE. It's a personal letter. (*Pause.*) I feel ill, I feel like
my vision's blurrin'.

LORRAINE *stares at the envelope.*

MARIE. Just open it for fuck's sake, you're making it worse.

LORRAINE. It's off Ben. I can feel it in here. He's only gone
and fucking written back, hasn't he? I didn't even think he'd
get it. I only wrote it for me coz that fucking speccy cunt told
me it'd help and now look what's happened.

MARIE. Lorraine, open it.

LORRAINE. I can't cope with this. You open it, please.

MARIE. It isn't mine. It isn't addressed to me.

LORRAINE. Please. Marie.

MARIE. What difference is it gonna make who opens it?

LORRAINE. I don't wanna see the words.

> LORRAINE *passes it to* MARIE.

MARIE. If he don't wanna see yer. I'm gonna feel like shit, Lorraine.

> *Pause.*

LORRAINE. Coming from you, hearing you say it... it'll make it a bit better.

> *Silence.* MARIE *goes to open the letter,* LORRAINE *puts her hand out.*

Oh, fuckin' hell, Marie.

MARIE. Do you want me to open it or what, Lorraine?

> LORRAINE *nods.* MARIE *opens it and reads.* LORRAINE *wrings her hands.*

LORRAINE. Oh fuckin' hell, Marie.

MARIE. It's off him. It's off Ben.

> *Silence.*

He wants to see you.

> *Silence.*

Lorraine? He wants to see yer.

> *Silence.* LORRAINE *takes the letter. She reads it then puts it down on the table. She is calm.*

LORRAINE. He wants to see me.

MARIE. That's brilliant. That's fuckin' …

Silence.

Lol?

Pause.

LORRAINE. I don't know what to do with myself.

MARIE. It's a good letter.

LORRAINE. Yeah.

MARIE. Do you want a drink? I got some vodka. Have a drink.

LORRAINE. I don't wanna drink.

LORRAINE *picks up the letter and reads it again.*

I'm gonna see my son. (*Beat.*) Aren't I?

MARIE. Yeah.

Scene Seven

Wednesday, midday. MARIE *is shutting the door. She comes back into the flat and sits down. She looks a little shaken. She sits down on the chair.* LORRAINE'*s holdall is on the floor. After a few seconds* LORRAINE'*s voice can be heard.*

LORRAINE. Marie? Can I come out now?

MARIE. Yeah. Yeah. (*Beat.*) Sorry.

LORRAINE *crawls out from under the couch bed.*

LORRAINE. My fucking back. Who was he?

MARIE. Bloke for the rent.

LORRAINE. Landlord?

MARIE. Yeah. Sort of.

LORRAINE. Why did it take so long?

MARIE *shrugs*.

MARIE. Just talkin'. He's alright. I'm sorry for making yer
hide.

LORRAINE. S'alright. (*Beat.*) Why did I have to hide?

MARIE. He'd get funny, that's all.

LORRAINE. I thought he was alright.

MARIE. He is… I'm just, not meant to have people round.

LORRAINE. You're not allowed to have guests?

MARIE. If he thought you were stayin' here. Sleepin' here.

LORRAINE. How would he know? I might've come for tea?
You can have people for tea. (*Beat.*) I could be yer fuckin'
mum. Free fucking country, you can't even have a mate
round for tea, what's that about?

MARIE. I know.

LORRAINE. Some people.

MARIE. Lol, I got you something. I got you a present.

LORRAINE. No… what'd you do that for?

MARIE. Coz I wanted to.

MARIE *gets a Peacocks' carrier bag from the back of the
door. She hands it to* LORRAINE. LORRAINE *reaches in
the bag and pulls out a flowery blouse. She holds it up.*

LORRAINE. Oh, that is… lovely. It's lovely, that is. It's… you
shouldn't have gone and done this.

MARIE. I thought you could wear it later.

LORRAINE. Well, this is it. I can wear it later, can't I?

MARIE. Do you like it?

LORRAINE. It's lovely.

MARIE. Try it on.

> LORRAINE *takes her sweatshirt off. She puts the blouse on but struggles to do up the top buttons, she manages but it gapes and strains across her chest.*

I wanted you to have something nice to wear.

LORRAINE. I can't – thank you. Thanks so much. Honestly, it's –

MARIE. Thought you can't turn up in your trackie, can yer?

LORRAINE. Well, this is it.

MARIE. Turn round.

> LORRAINE *turns round.* MARIE *stares for a few seconds.*

Is it a bit small?

LORRAINE. No… s'fine.

MARIE. It is a bit.

LORRAINE. It's mostly retention with me. I carry a lot of water.

MARIE. In your tits?

> MARIE *stands and goes over to* LORRAINE. *She undoes the top two buttons of the blouse.*

LORRAINE. Oh, hang on a minute, I'm not sure about that.

> MARIE *stands back to look.*

MARIE. Nah.

> LORRAINE *does herself back up. As she does so, a button pops off.*

LORRAINE. Oh fuckin'… beautiful.

> LORRAINE *hands the button to* MARIE *and starts to put her sweatshirt back on.*

MARIE. Kind of defeats the point, that, doesn't it?

LORRAINE. With me smart black slacks?

MARIE. Don't call 'em slacks, Lorraine… don't go saying things like slacks to him.

LORRAINE. They're not gonna come up much in conversation, are they? My trousers.

MARIE. I think they look weird with that jumper. It'll look weird.

LORRAINE. I don't think he's gonna care what I've got on, Marie.

LORRAINE *pulls the collar of the blouse out over the neck.*

How about that?

MARIE. I want you to look nice.

LORRAINE. Well, this is it, I wanna look nice but it isn't a fashion parade.

Pause.

MARIE. I want you to look like a mum.

LORRAINE. What's that meant to mean?

MARIE. You wore that jumper inside all the time.

Beat.

LORRAINE. So.

MARIE. So I just think… you can tell. (*Beat.*) You have an idea in your head. He might have an idea in his head. Of something, I dunno… what.

LORRAINE *takes the sweatshirt off.*

When I think of my mum I think she's wearing this beige sort of jacket… like a suit jacket but not so… it's linen. From Marks an' Sparks or Principles and she's got a dotty navy blouse underneath and a nice skirt that sort of flares out.

LORRAINE. I've only got jumpers.

MARIE. Put your mac on.

LORRAINE. What if we go indoors?

MARIE. Keep it on.

LORRAINE. That's ridiculous. I'll look like fuckin' Inspector Clouseau.

MARIE. Just... not the jumper.

LORRAINE *unbuttons the blouse, revealing a black vest top underneath.*

See... that's perfect. You look really smart.

LORRAINE. Well, this is it. I feel... presentable. S'like that programme where those two women take some shitty-looking article off the street and put them in something they can't afford. (*Beat.*) Yeah, I'm happy with that.

MARIE *gets a mini sewing kit from the drawer. She starts to sew the button back on.*

Feels funny, this. You sewing my button on. (*Beat.*) He used to bite his. Was always suckin' them. He had this duffel coat when he was about six. Buttons like brazil nuts. It was either blue or brown. (*Pause.*) I torture myself sometimes with that. That I can't remember whether it was blue or brown. (*Beat.*) Anyway, it was a blue or brown duffel coat. We went the shop and he picked it. First time he'd ever chosen anything on his own. I wanted him to get a little ski jacket. One of them you can just bang in the machine and it dries dead quick. (*Beat.*) Don't you go jabbing my tit.

MARIE. Keep still then... jigglin' about.

LORRAINE *stands perfectly still.* MARIE *sews. Silence.*

LORRAINE. But I'd promised y'see. Before we left home I had said he could choose one all by himself and as soon as we get in there he marches straight over, like a little soldier all straight-backed and determined, he marches over to this rack of duffel coats and he asks me which one is his size and I look at the hangers and pull it out and he puts it on and won't take it off. He says, 'This is my winter coat.' He looked like an evacuee. He said it was the best coat he'd ever had.

He slept in it that night with the hood up. I went in and sat on his bed and fuckin' broke my heart crying.

He wore it on the day they came for him. And a hat. A knitted hat. It was definitely red that hat. (*Beat*.) And gloves. Mittens with the strings that run right through.

We stood there.

We stood there together and I put my hand out and he put his hand out and we held hands.

Pause.

I asked if he was cold and he said no. Then the woman came in and he had to go.

Silence.

I think it was brown. I think it was definitely brown, y'know? When I shut my eyes I can smell him. I can smell the smell of him going. It's like bedclothes and plasticine and gumdrops.

MARIE *finishes and bites the thread off.*

MARIE. I'll do yer hair for yer as well. Blow-dried or something. Cut it maybe. S'a bit... innit?

LORRAINE. Sod right off. You're not cuttin' my hair. You can put it up for me but you're not fuckin' cutting it.

MARIE. I could do a roll or something. All piled up at the back and turned under like a French pleat.

LORRAINE. I'm not Margot fucking Fonteyn, Marie. (*Beat*.) I wanna feel comfortable. Just wanna be meself.

MARIE. I'm talking about sticking yer hair up, not having a facelift.

LORRAINE. When he was little I used to plait it. He liked it like that.

MARIE. He's not little any more, though, is he? And you was younger then, Lorraine.

Silence.

LORRAINE. I'm gonna take this off now. I don't wanna spill anything on it.

LORRAINE *starts getting changed back into her tracksuit.*

What time is it?

MARIE. Ten past twelve.

Pause.

LORRAINE. Four hours and fifty minutes.

MARIE. You know where you're going?

LORRAINE. Yes.

MARIE. Give yourself plenty of time. In case you get lost.

LORRAINE *nods. Silence.*

LORRAINE. I got butterflies.

MARIE. You will have.

LORRAINE. I worry sometimes that he'll have forgotten us. What we were like. Together. But then I think he was seven when he went. That's not a baby, seven, is it? You remember things from seven easy. My first memory's of being on one of them tiny little donkeys on the beach. We all got taken out on one of them buses. I'm wearing a little blue smocky dress thing and I swear I'm not older than about three. (*Beat.*) I've still got the photo somewhere.

Scene Eight

Night. The flat is a bit of a mess. The table is littered with beer cans, a vodka bottle, pizza boxes and crisp packets. MARIE *and* LORRAINE *sit, drinking.* MARIE *is smoking.*

LORRAINE. He was lovely. He looked lovely.

Pause.

He had... I looked in his eyes and they were just exactly the same. Like conkers. All dark and round and shiny. He let me stare at him which I thought was good of him, wasn't it? Just letting me stare like that. He's got a lovely flat. All brown leather and big... whatsits, lampshades. We sat on the couch and he made some tea and he just let me stare. (*Beat.*) Beautiful dark hair.

MARIE. You must've said something.

LORRAINE. Oh God, yeah. This is it. Yes. We said lots of something. Things. We said a lot of stuff. And he wasn't... I said, 'I know you must be angry. You must have a hell of a lot of anger. Don't hold back.' But he said he didn't, he said he wasn't angry. And he even let me hold his hand. I think he must be some sort of angel, letting me do that. Letting me stride in there and stare at him and hold his hand.

MARIE. What does he do?

Pause.

LORRAINE. He's a teacher. He teaches in a... school.

MARIE. That's good. That's a nice job, eh?

LORRAINE. They call him Mr Hibbens.

MARIE. That's his name?

LORRAINE. Well... yeah, course it is.

MARIE. He kept it. He kept your name.

Beat.

LORRAINE. Yeah.

Pause.

MARIE. What's he teach?

LORRAINE (*thinks*). I forgot. I forgot to ask him. That's terrible. I didn't even ask him what he teaches.

MARIE. You can ask him next time.

LORRAINE. This is it. I'm gonna have to write a list. A list of things to ask. D'you think?

Pause.

MARIE. Nah. Bit weird, innit? Rocking up with a big fuckin' questionnaire. He'll think you're mad.

LORRAINE. I won't get it out. I won't read it out to him. I'll learn all the questions and drop them into the conversation. (*Beat.*) Number one, what d'you teach?

MARIE. Has he got a girlfriend?

LORRAINE. Number two, have you got a girlfriend? (*Beat.*) No, he has a got a girlfriend. He said. She's called Claire.

MARIE. What does she do, then? Claire.

LORRAINE. I can't remember. I'll put it on me list.

Silence.

MARIE. Did he talk about his parents?

Pause.

LORRAINE. His... the... she's dead and he, his... dad lives in... Spain.

Silence.

He's got a house there apparently. A 'villa'.

MARIE. When did his mum die?

Pause.

LORRAINE. Last year. (*Beat.*) I don't think he was that close to her from what I could gather. I didn't think they were that close. It didn't seem like it.

Silence.

MARIE. When are you gonna see him again?

LORRAINE. He's asked me round for tea. In a couple of days.

MARIE. Right. He's keen. (*Beat.*) That's brilliant, that is, Lorraine.

LORRAINE. I know. (*Beat.*) It's brilliant. I know. I can't hardly believe it.

MARIE. I bet you can't.

MARIE *passes another can to* LORRAINE.

LORRAINE. You shouldn't have gone and done all this, Marie. Please let me give you some of my money.

MARIE. I don't want your money, Lorraine.

LORRAINE. You've spent a fortune –

MARIE. I got paid today. Lol, there might be a job. At the pub. They said they might have one.

LORRAINE. Really?

MARIE. This woman reckons she might be leaving. She's not sure yet because it all depends on this bloke. Her fella. And whether he has to move to Manchester with work. She'll go with him you see. If he goes. (*Beat.*) She's gonna let me know. I spoke to the manager. Said you'd be perfect for it. Didn't tell him about you being inside obviously. He seemed keen.

LORRAINE. Did he?

MARIE. Yeah. She's going to tell me soon. This woman. Once she knows about her fella's job.

LORRAINE. What's her name?

MARIE. Gillian.

LORRAINE. Gillian. (*Beat*.) I'll get her a thank-you card.

MARIE. Hang on. See what happens first.

LORRAINE. When will she know?

MARIE. I don't know. Soon.

LORRAINE. Soon. (*Beat*.) I'll try not to think about it too
    much.

MARIE. Yeah.

LORRAINE. Is it Gillian with a G or a J?

MARIE. I don't know, I'll ask her.

LORRAINE. That'd be a laugh, wouldn't it? Me and you
    working together.

MARIE. Let's play floppy dollies.

LORRAINE. Oh, Marie, no.

MARIE. Why not?

LORRAINE. Coz it's just – it's fuckin' daft.

MARIE. That's the whole point.

LORRAINE. No.

MARIE. Go on. I used to love doin' floppy dollies.

LORRAINE. I haven't got the energy.

MARIE. Don't be a boring cunt, Lol.

    MARIE *goes into the kitchen, gets a tea towel and hands it
    to* LORRAINE, *who ties it around* MARIE's *head*.

LORRAINE. You can't see nothin'?

MARIE. Course I can't.

LORRAINE. Alright.

    LORRAINE *twirls her around a few times*.

MARIE. Easy. Fuckin' hell.

LORRAINE. Alright. Lie down.

> MARIE *lowers herself onto the floor then lies flat out.*
> LORRAINE *then grabs hold of her ankles and starts to pull her.*

Jesus, you've put some weight on, girl.

> LORRAINE *pulls and starts to drag* MARIE *around the room, disorientating her. They are both laughing uncontrollably. After a while* LORRAINE *stops by the door to the flat and lowers* MARIE's *legs. She is puffed out.*

Alright. Tell me where you are.

Pause.

MARIE. Right next to the bathroom.

LORRAINE. Take it off.

> MARIE *takes off the blindfold.*

You never do it, do yer? You never get it right.

MARIE. You fuckin' try it, it's hard.

LORRAINE. Shut up, you're not doing it to me.

MARIE. Go on.

LORRAINE. You couldn't lift my foot, let alone drag me round the bloody room.

MARIE. I could, I'm really strong now.

> MARIE *starts putting the blindfold on* LORRAINE.

LORRAINE. No way.

MARIE. Shut up.

> MARIE *starts twirling* LORRAINE *round. She shrieks with laughter.*

LORRAINE. I'll be sick.

MARIE. Right, now lie down.

LORRAINE. You be careful with my legs. I get neuralgia.

MARIE. You don't get neuralgia in yer fuckin' legs, Lorraine. Neuralgia's a headache.

MARIE *starts to pull both* LORRAINE*'s legs. It's a massive effort and both women are soon laughing helplessly.* MARIE *manages to drag her a little way across the room before collapsing next to her.*

Fuckin' hell, Lorraine, have you got steel weights down your pants?

LORRAINE. I'm heavy-boned. Jesus, I feel pissed.

MARIE. You've only had two cans.

LORRAINE. Two cans more than I've had in… years. First time in… I'll be on me back.

MARIE. It's a celebration.

LORRAINE. I need to pace myself. I shouldn't be getting drunk, not with my tablets.

LORRAINE *gets her tablets out and starts to read the packet.* MARIE *reaches over and swipes them away. She stands holding them out of* LORRAINE*'s reach.*

MARIE. You should knock these on the head now, Lol.

LORRAINE. They say you shouldn't just stop taking them. They say you've got to do it slowly.

MARIE. Who's 'they', then? Eh? Some big fat fucking pharmaceutical company? Course they say that. They don't want you to stop, do they?

LORRAINE. I gotta wean myself off.

MARIE. That's what they say. They say that but you've just got to knock it on the head.

LORRAINE. Can I have them back, Marie?

MARIE. You've got to start as you mean to go on.

LORRAINE. I am. I'm weaning myself off.

MARIE. I didn't do that. I didn't 'wean' myself, Lorraine. I just packed it all in. And look how I'm doing.

LORRAINE. I just want to do it my way. Can I have them back?

LORRAINE *steps forward,* MARIE *holds the tablets out of her reach.*

MARIE. I'm looking out for you.

LORRAINE. You're not. You're in one of your funny moods.

MARIE. Oh right, thanks. That's fucking gratitude for you, isn't it? I'm helping you out here and you're calling me a fucking moody cunt.

LORRAINE. I'm not calling you anything.

MARIE. I'll give you these back but only if you swear you're gonna go and flush them down the bog, Lorraine.

LORRAINE. Just give me them back.

MARIE. Will you go and flush them down the toilet, Lorraine?

LORRAINE. No.

MARIE. Am I gonna have to flush them down the toilet, Lorraine?

LORRAINE. Don't you dare.

MARIE. This is why you're always asleep though. Coz of these fucking things. You can't be an astronaut if you're fucking dropping off every five minutes.

LORRAINE *snaps. She moves quickly and grabs the tablets out of* MARIE*'s hand.*

LORRAINE (*screaming in* MARIE*'s face*). Fucking give them back.

MARIE. Easy.

LORRAINE *sits down. She is flustered and upset.*

LORRAINE. Sorry. I didn't mean to get – but you wind me up sometimes. Marie. I don't think it's fair, you know what you're doing.

MARIE. Come off it.

LORRAINE. You get me so I can't think straight sometimes. You have this… way. This knack. It makes me nervous.

Pause. LORRAINE *takes two tablets from a strip and swallows them with water.*

MARIE. So what happens then? With the tablets. Coming off them. Weaning yourself.

Pause.

LORRAINE. Next week I take one and three-quarters for a month. Then I take one and a half the next month. Month after that I take one and a quarter. Then one. Then half. Then a quarter. Then an eighth. Then I stop.

MARIE. That's good, then, isn't it?

LORRAINE *nods.*

LORRAINE. I frightened you then?

MARIE. Made me fucking jump a bit.

LORRAINE. It's only me, Marie.

MARIE. I know.

LORRAINE. What did you think I was gonna do?

MARIE. Nothing. You made me jump. That's all. I wound you up.

Silence.

What did it feel like?

LORRAINE. What did what feel like?

MARIE. Killing someone.

Silence.

Fuck. I'm sorry.

Pause.

LORRAINE. It was easy.

Silence.

It was easy. (*Pause.*) He had a thin shirt on. He had his leather jacket over his shoulder. If he'd had that on it might have been much more – It just sort of slid in. My hand was bleeding quite badly from where I'd smashed the bottle on the table but I didn't notice 'til afterwards. They had some police nurse stitch it up for me. Only young she was. I felt sorry for her. I go, 'You should be out with your friends tonight,' and she smiled at me. She was nice.

Silence. MARIE *opens another can for herself.*

MARIE. Shall we put some music on? We could have a dance.

LORRAINE. …

MARIE. C'mon, Lol.

LORRAINE. I don't feel like it.

MARIE. You will do when you get going. Hang on.

MARIE *roots in her CD box and brings out a CD. She shows it to* LORRAINE.

It's your favourite song.

LORRAINE. One of them. It is. Yeah, one of my favourites.

MARIE. I remember you tellin' me that. You were looking after me. Bein' lovely when I was freakin' out and you said it cheered you up when you was sad.

LORRAINE. It does, yeah. It cheers me up when I'm a bit…

MARIE. I bought it when I got out. I went and bought it coz of what you said. How much you liked listening to it.

LORRAINE. I'll sit and listen but I haven't danced to it before.

MARIE. You only don't dance, Lorraine, coz you've had no reason to for fucking... twelve years.

LORRAINE. I didn't really even do it before, though. I just... I'm not a dancer.

MARIE *puts the CD on: Creedence Clearwater Revival's 'It's Just A Thought'. She turns the volume right up and drags* LORRAINE *up.* MARIE *is a good dancer.* LORRAINE *is terrible and very self-conscious at first until she notices that* MARIE *isn't taking much notice of her. She loosens up a bit and starts to go a bit mad, jumping around, not remotely in time to the music.* MARIE *notices now and starts to laugh.* LORRAINE *carries on, showing off a bit. Suddenly she stops and sinks onto the couch.* MARIE *turns the music off.*

MARIE. You alright?

LORRAINE. Yeah, I feel a bit – (*She exhales deeply.*) I think I'm gonna throw up.

LORRAINE *stands up, before she makes it to the loo, she is violently sick on the floor.* MARIE *looks away.*

I'm sorry.

MARIE. I'll clean it up. D'you wanna glass of water?

LORRAINE. I'll do it, please I – I don't want you – I don't want you to do it, please I feel. Embarrassed.

LORRAINE *starts to cry.*

MARIE. Oh, shut up, Lorraine. You threw up. Big deal.

MARIE *sits down and puts her arm around* LORRAINE. *She is sobbing now.*

Lorraine, c'mon, it's a bit of puke. Bit of fuckin'... sick on the floor. Crap party if no one throws up on the carpet, innit?

LORRAINE (*nods*). I'm alright now. Sobered up n'all.

LORRAINE *blows her nose. There is a long silence as* MARIE *sits with her arm around her.*

MARIE. Are you gonna clean it up, then? I mean, I'll do it, I don't mind, but we don't wanna just leave it there. Gets a bit...

LORRAINE. Yeah. Sorry, yeah.

LORRAINE *gets up and goes into the kitchen.* MARIE *goes to the CD player and puts the music back on low. She lights another cigarette.* LORRAINE *comes back in with a cloth and spray. She gets to work, scrubbing on her hands and knees.* MARIE *turns the volume up again and starts dancing.* LORRAINE *carries on scrubbing.*

Scene Nine

Thursday, 7 a.m. The flat is a mess. LORRAINE *is sleeping.* MARIE *enters, dressed in the same clothes as the previous night. She tiptoes in quietly, but* LORRAINE *is already awake. She sits up in bed.*

LORRAINE. Marie, where've you been?

MARIE. Shop.

LORRAINE. It's seven o'clock. What did yer need from the shops so desperate?

MARIE. Tampax.

LORRAINE. You got Tampax in the bathroom.

MARIE. I needed Super.

LORRAINE. You've been gone all night.

MARIE. No I haven't.

LORRAINE. I woke up about four and you weren't in bed.

MARIE. Must have been in the toilet.

LORRAINE. You weren't. I looked. I've been out me mind. (*Beat.*) Marie, where've you been to?

Beat.

MARIE. A party.

LORRAINE. Whose party?

MARIE. A mate's.

LORRAINE. You should have let me know.

MARIE. Well, I would have done if you hadn't been in a fuckin' coma by half past ten.

Pause.

LORRAINE. Why didn't you say that then? Why didn't you say you'd been to a party when I asked?

MARIE. Oh, for fuck's sake, Lorraine. Because I know what you get like. Giving me earache about going out late at night on me own.

LORRAINE. You shouldn't go out late at night on your own.

MARIE. See?

MARIE *goes to the kitchen cupboard. She comes out with two cans of lager. She opens one, takes a swig and offers the other to* LORRAINE.

Hair of the dog.

LORRAINE. I don't know how you can do that.

MARIE *clambers onto the bed next to* LORRAINE.

MARIE. Lorraine. I wanna get away. D'you still wanna go somewhere?

LORRAINE. What d'you mean?

MARIE. Little holiday. Me and you. We'll just get a coach somewhere.

LORRAINE. When?

MARIE. Now.

LORRAINE. This minute?

MARIE. Yeah.

LORRAINE. Why the rush?

MARIE. Why not?

LORRAINE. It's a bit… unexpected.

MARIE. What, your affairs not in order or something? You not finished highlighting the rest of the week's telly in the *TV Quick?* (*Beat*.) Just stick a pair of knickers in a bag. Get a B&B. Go and sit on the beach –

LORRAINE. It's raining.

MARIE. Go and sit in a fucking pub, then. This was your idea, Lorraine.

LORRAINE. I know.

MARIE. Right then. Get ready.

LORRAINE. Not… now though. Not straight away.

MARIE. Why not?

LORRAINE. I just need a bit of time. Get me head round it. Feels a bit… sudden.

MARIE. I'm talking about going to Brighton for two nights not fucking emigrating to Australia. (*Beat*.) When was the last time you did something spontaneous, Lorraine?

LORRAINE. I'm not s'posed to go on holiday yet, am I?

MARIE. Oh, fuck them, Lol. You're a free woman now. What about the sand between your toes… all that?

LORRAINE. I do want to. I'd love it, Marie. More than anything. Just need to get geared up first, that's all.

MARIE *swigs the can down.*

You want to watch that. Drinking like that.

MARIE. Do you wanna go away or what, Lorraine?

Pause.

LORRAINE. I don't feel ready.

MARIE. Please yerself.

LORRAINE. Don't be like that.

MARIE. I'm not being like anything. Don't make no difference to me, Lorraine. I'm trying to do you a favour, that's all.

LORRAINE. We could go next week maybe.

Silence.

Couldn't we?

MARIE. Yeah.

MARIE starts to get undressed. She goes into the bathroom and gets into the shower.

LORRAINE (*shouting*). That'd be lovely, that.

LORRAINE gets out of bed, sits in the chair and switches the TV on.

Scene Ten

Friday night. MARIE's flat is tidy. The door opens slowly and MARIE limps in holding a chip-shop bag. Her jacket is ripped and her face is bruised and cut. Blood runs from a cut on her knee and she clutches her side. She sits down in the chair and puts her head in her hands.

LORRAINE enters from the bathroom. She is holding a sponge and some bath cleaner. She stops and stares in horrified silence at MARIE.

LORRAINE *drops the sponge and the cleaner and goes to*
MARIE. LORRAINE *puts her arms around* MARIE. MARIE
brushes her off.

MARIE. I'm alright.

LORRAINE. Jesus.

MARIE. I'm alright.

LORRAINE. Look at you. What happened?

MARIE. I'm alright.

LORRAINE. You're not alright. Stop sayin' you're alright.
   You're not alright. Oh, fucking hell, Marie, what's going
   on?

MARIE. I got us chips from the chippy.

LORRAINE. Oh Jesus.

MARIE. How did it go with Ben?

LORRAINE. I want to get hold of you.

MARIE. I don't want you to fucking get hold of me, I want you
   to tell me about Ben. (*Beat.*) Did he let you stare again?

   LORRAINE *nods.*

   Hold his hand?

   LORRAINE *nods.*

   He's a fucking little diamond, he is, isn't he?

   Silence.

   Isn't he, though? He sounds great. Do you think he likes this
   girl, then? Claire. Coz if he's not that into her, you could put
   a good word in for me, couldn't yer? Yeah? Set us up.

LORRAINE. Can I please go and get a cloth for your face?

MARIE. I don't want a cloth for my face.

LORRAINE. What happened?

MARIE. I got us some chips. I wasn't sure whether you wanted gravy or not. I know what you're like about gravy, you gotta be in the mood, haven't you, Lorraine? Gravy and Mars Bars. I got a separate tub anyway. I thought we could share it.

Silence.

Plates or out the paper? We should get plates really, shouldn't we, or the gravy'll go everywhere. (*Beat.*) Could you go and get some plates, then?

LORRAINE *stands, shaken. She puts the wrapped chips on the plates and gets two forks. She hands a plate to* MARIE. *They sit on the floor next to each other.* MARIE *divides the chips up. She opens the tub of gravy and holds it up.*

Are you in the mood today, Lorraine?

LORRAINE. Yes. Please.

MARIE *pours the gravy on both plates.*

Thank you.

MARIE. You're very welcome.

They sit in silence with the plates on their laps but neither of them touch the food.

LORRAINE. I went to your pub today, Marie.

Silence.

The Windmill on Brixton Hill. They said you haven't been working there for six months.

Silence.

MARIE. Why are you spying on me, Lorraine?

LORRAINE. I wasn't spying on you. I wanted to talk to you about something.

MARIE. Couldn't it have waited?

LORRAINE. No. It was about going to Ben's.

MARIE. Did you show yourself up, Lorraine? Did you tread dog shit on his nice cream carpet?

LORRAINE. I spoke to that lad you told me about. Your manager. (*Beat*.) I wanted to punch him in the face. Way he looked at me. Little prick.

Silence.

That wasn't true, then, was it? About Gillian moving to Manchester with her boyfriend?

MARIE. There wasn't even a fucking Gillian worked there when I did. I made her up. (*Pause*.) I liked seeing you excited. Sorry.

LORRAINE. Where've you been, Marie?

LORRAINE *sits with the plate on her lap, staring at* MARIE*'s face*. MARIE *puts a chip in her mouth*.

MARIE. They're cold.

MARIE *starts to sob, huge racking sobs*. LORRAINE *puts her plate down and holds her*.

LORRAINE. What happened?

MARIE. Please stop saying that.

LORRAINE. I wanna know. Who did this to yer?

MARIE. Why? So you can go and bottle them? (*Beat*.) I don't think that's the way forward, Lorraine. I don't think that fucking solves things.

LORRAINE. That's not fair.

MARIE. You don't half talk some rubbish sometimes, Lorraine. Do you ever listen to yourself? You should get one of them things, one of them whatsits… dictaphones. You should tape yourself having a conversation with someone, then you should play it back. Listen to yourself. To what you say. It's meaningless a lot of the time.

Silence.

I'm not being nasty, it just gets on my tits.

Silence.

'This is it,' about every fucking thing. I wanna scream in
your face, 'What is fucking what?' 'I'm gonna go the shop,
Lorraine, get a bit of fresh air.' 'Well, this is it.' 'I might go
to bed now, get an early night.' 'Well, this is it.' 'I want to
fucking kill myself.' 'Well, this is it.' What is fucking what,
Lorraine? What is fucking what? What is what?

LORRAINE. I'm ringing the police.

MARIE *starts laughing.*

What?

MARIE. You just make me fucking… howl sometimes, Lorraine.
Yeah go on. Ring the police for us, will yer? Perfect.

LORRAINE. Are you pissed?

MARIE. Luckily, I am a bit, yeah. (*Beat.*) This little kid, comes
up to me when I'm waiting for the chips. Asks if I'll go the
shop next door and get four bottles of Blackthorn for him an'
his mates. Says he'll keep me place in the queue. Calls me
'love'. 'Oh, go on, love.' He's about… twelve.

LORRAINE. Did he do this?

MARIE. No. Course he didn't. I sat in the park with them. They
made me laugh. I felt like a kid myself. (*Beat.*) I think most
kids are alright these days. You always hear stuff but most of
them are alright I think. They were alright. There was this
little one and he had his toe sticking out of his trainer. That
fuckin'… that did me in, that. He weren't wearing any socks.
(*Beat.*) Most days something happens… something happens
which just fucking breaks my heart. I can be feeling alright
or fucking indifferent or whatever and then I walk past
McDonald's and there's an old woman on her own eating a
hamburger and it'll just do me right in. Little papery hands
like birds' feet. Most days I just can't take one small thing in
this fuckin' world.

LORRAINE. We'll be alright, you and me, Marie. We will.

MARIE. Why d'you keep doin' that, Lorraine? Why d'you keep sayin' 'we' and 'you and me'? There is no fuckin' 'you and me'.

LORRAINE. Course there is… what you saying that for? I love you.

MARIE. Oh, Lorraine, stop it, you make me feel fuckin' – you creep me out when you say you love me. You don't even fucking know me.

LORRAINE. Don't say that, Marie, don't say that.

MARIE. Love. You aren't my fucking mother, Lorraine, or my fucking… girlfriend.

LORRAINE. Marie, stop it don't say stuff like – We're mates –

MARIE. Yeah, well, 'mates' don't spend every fucking second of every fucking day together, Lorraine. They don't sleep in the same fucking room night after endless night, talking about everything under the sun apart from what the fuck they're gonna do with their miserable fucking lives.

LORRAINE. There's things to look forward to. Things to hope for.

MARIE. Like fucking what exactly?

LORRAINE. …

MARIE. I'm no good at this. I'm no good at it. I am no good at getting through the fuckin' day, Lorraine. Never mind getting through life. Never mind making plans and actually seeing them through.

LORRAINE. You're in shock.

MARIE. Too fucking right I'm in shock. I've been in fucking shock since the second I was born. And I'm sick of it. I'm sick of being frightened. I live in fear. Fear of going to sleep at night. Fear of waking up. Fear of someone knocking on the door. Fear of the fucking shops.

I'm so afraid of the shops. I am so frightened of rows and rows and rows.

Beat.

And crowds. Fear of crowds. Fear of empty rooms. Fear of being away from home even though I haven't got one.

Beat.

Fear of being left.

LORRAINE. I wouldn't leave yer. (*Beat.*) I won't leave yer.

Silence.

MARIE. I don't want you here any more, Lorraine. I want you to go. I can't sort myself out, let alone you.

LORRAINE. I don't want you to sort me out. I just want us to carry on being what we are.

MARIE. And what is that, Lorraine? What exactly are we? You think you can just fuckin' – I'm fuckin' puttin' you up. Puttin' food in your fat frightened gob. I can't give you anything any more.

LORRAINE. I don't want anything.

MARIE. What is it gonna take? Lorraine. What is it gonna take for you to just leave me alone?

LORRAINE. When you tell me you're alright.

MARIE. Do I look alright? Lorraine? Do I fucking look alright?

LORRAINE. No.

MARIE *throws the plate of chips and lets out a cry of frustration.*

MARIE. Why won't you fucking leave me alone? Go on, fuck off.

MARIE *stands and starts to push* LORRAINE *towards the door.* LORRAINE *resists as* MARIE *continues.* MARIE *pushes harder and* LORRAINE *grabs hold of her hands.*

MARIE *pulls away and hits* LORRAINE *hard, knocking her glasses off.* LORRAINE *puts her hand to her face.* MARIE *stops then slumps to the floor in a heap sobbing.*
LORRAINE *calmly picks her glasses from the floor and puts them back on, then she bends down and cradles* MARIE. MARIE *puts her arms around* LORRAINE. *She is sobbing loudly.* LORRAINE *strokes her hair and rocks her.*

I'm sorry.

LORRAINE. It's alright.

MARIE. I want my mum.

LORRAINE. I've got yer.

MARIE. I'm sorry.

LORRAINE. I've got yer.

Silence. MARIE *composes herself.*

MARIE. I have this dream about her. (*Pause.*) I'm a little girl. I'm in my nightie and I'm lying on a carpet underneath a huge skylight. I'm looking up, my arms like this, stretching. Wanting to be picked up.

I know she's through the skylight somewhere but I can't see her. I can't hear her voice either but I know what she's saying. I feel winded. I can feel the carpet itching through my nightie and I look up and sunlight pours in even though it's gone midnight and I stop itching and just soak it up. Feel it on my face and on my belly like she's blowing raspberries on it. (*Beat.*) I'm glad you found Ben, Lorraine. I'm glad you found him. I'm sorry.

LORRAINE. It's alright.

MARIE. I'm glad you get that chance.

Silence.

LORRAINE. That's what I wanted to talk to you about. He doesn't want to see me. Doesn't want nothing to do with me.

MARIE. He wrote you a letter. I read it. You met him. He let you hold his hand.

LORRAINE. Yeah. (*Pause*.) He was nice. He wasn't not nice. He just said that he 'couldn't envisage us having a relationship'. He didn't think it was possible after everything. He said he just wanted to see me once because he had a lot to deal with. In his head. He thought it might help. Seeing me. Drawing a line. He said things like they do on the telly. Closure. (*Beat*.) I let him speak and then we left each other. I didn't say much because it didn't seem fair. He'd made his mind up. You have to respect that, don't yer? (*Beat*.) You have to respect it.

MARIE *pulls away from* LORRAINE *then wraps her arms around her. They hold each other.*

Scene Eleven

The following morning. MARIE *sits reading* LORRAINE*'s book in the chair.* LORRAINE *enters, she stands watching* MARIE. MARIE *continues to read in silence for a while before speaking.*

MARIE. 'The Earth's revolution time increases .0001 seconds annually.' We just keep spinning round faster and faster. (*Beat*.) You should highlight that, Lorraine.

LORRAINE. Think I'm all done now.

MARIE. 'One day on Pluto is about the length of one week on Earth.'

LORRAINE. Thank God I didn't get sent down on fucking Pluto.

MARIE *bursts out laughing.*

What?

MARIE. You fucking crack me up.

LORRAINE. Do I?

Pause. MARIE *continues reading.*

MARIE. Course you do. You know you do.

LORRAINE. Marie, I'm ready.

MARIE. 'If you shouted in space, even if someone was standing right next to you they wouldn't be able to hear you.'

LORRAINE. And on Earth most of the fucking time.

LORRAINE *sits on the edge of the bed.*

MARIE. 'If you attempted to count all the stars in a galaxy at a rate of one every second it would take 3,000 years to count them all.' *(Beat.)* It's got a little fact section at the back. It's good, this, isn't it?

MARIE *looks up at* LORRAINE *for the first time. They take each other in.*

LORRAINE. You can have that. I'll leave it here.

Silence.

MARIE. I'm so sorry I stopped coming in. I hated it.

LORRAINE. That's alright... Jesus, that's okay. Fuckin' hell, you've just got shot of the place, you don't wanna be back in there every five minutes, do yer? Gotta get on with things.

MARIE. I hated it mostly because I sort of missed it. *(Beat.)* Or I missed you.

LORRAINE. Yeah?

Silence. LORRAINE *pulls another letter from her bag and hands it to* MARIE.

That's Ben's letter. From under me pillow. If I keep it it's gonna do me in. I might rip it up and that'd... it'd break my heart. I can't look at it any more. I just want it to be safe.

MARIE *takes the letter.*

Read it if yer like.

MARIE. No.

LORRAINE. I want yer to.

Pause. MARIE reads.

He was six, you can't make it out really.

MARIE. No... you can. He's got good writing. Clever.

LORRAINE. Isn't he?

Silence.

I'm gonna go now, Marie.

MARIE. It's awful out.

LORRAINE *picks her bag up, puts her coat on.* LORRAINE *gives* MARIE *a quick kiss,* MARIE *tries to hold onto to her but she pulls away.*

LORRAINE. Take care of yourself, won't yer? (*Beat.*) Promise me.

MARIE. Yeah.

LORRAINE. I'll see you somewhere soon.

LORRAINE *leaves.* MARIE *takes the letter and sits. She reads it through before curling up in a ball. Suddenly there is a loud knock at the door.* MARIE *jumps up and opens it.* LORRAINE *bursts in, soaking wet.*

Can I borrow a brolly? It's cats and dogs out there. Need windscreen wipers for me gigs.

LORRAINE *takes her glasses off.*

MARIE. I haven't got a brolly.

LORRAINE. Alright. I'll – I just thought.

She turns to go.

MARIE. Lorraine. (*Pause.*) Stay. (*Beat.*) 'Til it stops.

Pause.

LORRAINE. Just 'til it eases off.

MARIE. Yeah.

LORRAINE takes her coat off. MARIE takes it from her.

LORRAINE. Thank you.

MARIE hangs the coat up. LORRAINE wanders over to the window. She looks out into next door's garden.

Oi, Mickey, ten out of ten for perseverance.

MARIE comes out of the kitchen and leans against the door and watches LORRAINE before joining her at the window. They stand together in silence for a few moments.

It's stopped rainin'.

MARIE. Has it?

They stay where they are.

The End.

A Nick Hern Book

This Wide Night first published in Great Britain as a paperback original in 2008 by Nick Hern Books Limited, The Glasshouse, 49a Goldhawk Road, London W12 8QP, in association with Clean Break

This revised edition published in 2009
Reprinted 2010, 2011, 2012

This Wide Night copyright © 2008, 2009 Chloë Moss

Chloë Moss has asserted her right to be identified as the author of this work

Cover image © Nan Goldin, 'Self-portrait in Blue Bathroom', London 1980, from *The Ballad of Sexual Dependency*
Cover design by Ned Hoste, 2H

Typeset by Nick Hern Books, London
Printed and bound in Great Britain by Mimeo Ltd, Huntingdon, Cambridgeshire PE29 6XX

A CIP catalogue record for this book is available from the British Library

ISBN 978 1 84842 002 1